MOMENTS IN TIME

LINDA KOEPPEL

MOMENTS IN TIME

iUniverse books may be ordered through booksellers or by contacting:

iUniverse
1663 Liberty Drive
Bloomington, IN 47403
www.iuniverse.com
844-349-9409

ISBN: 978-1-6632-4134-4 (sc)
ISBN: 978-1-6632-4135-1 (e)

Print information available on the last page.

iUniverse rev. date: 01/12/2023

CHAPTER 1

***

Directly Direct

It was the year of 2020. It was supposed to be an exciting year. That was before Covid hit planet Earth. Some people believed it was the beginning of the end of the world. Other people thought the virus was no bigger deal than other situations our country had been through and survived, only to come out of it a stronger nation.

What I knew was the stores were open only under certain circumstances. Churches were empty on Sunday and all other days of the week. The unbelievable happened when baseball season was cancelled. I knew it was serious when the government found it necessary to put out a stay-at-home order. The whole second half of school was canceled which meant there may not be any graduation ceremonies for school seniors. Nursing homes were locked down and visitation was forbidden. Only life-threatening health issues were allowed to be admitted to the hospital. Certain factories were shut down and thousands of people were left unemployed. I was not sure what it all meant except I knew it meant something serious was happening and the population of the whole world was at risk.

Schools being shut down meant children were at home.

It became the parent's responsibility to teach children their schoolwork on the computer. Some parents chose to make the uncertain situation into as much of a positive situation as possible. One mother took three weeks off with pay and stayed at home with her children. Every day she had specific activities planned for her children to do. As much as humanly possible she made sure her children did not get bored at home. Another mother worked two jobs which did not allow her to be home as much as she wanted to be. She was a single mom and could not afford the luxury of having just one full time job. Having the second job was not an option. It was a necessity. When this mom was able to be home, they spent time cuddling and watching television together, as long as the children got their schoolwork done for the day. Her children were older and could be counted on to be on their own when it was required. Another mother worked with senior patients at their homes. This left her a small amount of flexibility in her scheduled work time, to be home with her children during the pandemic break out.

It was not just the single mothers who struggled. Two parent families struggled with going to their job, helping with home schoolwork, running to the grocery stores in an attempt to find the items needed for their home food pantry. Most stores had limits on what you could take as well or how much you could take. For a while you were lucky if there were any groceries on the shelf.

I guess I should have not been so selfish during this time

when our nation needed people to step up and pull together to bring us out alive. I kept seeing pictures of young nurses, paramedics, and many health care workers who had a career of caring for sick patients while trying to protect themselves from the virus but to no avail. Some would even lose their own lives helping others to live. It was tragic, and it was scary for me to read those stories.

Now comes the I feel sorry for me part. One of my granddaughters worked in our local hospital in the Emergency Room while finishing up nursing school. Another worked at the same hospital while she attended nursing school as well. Another granddaughter worked in a nursing home taking care of the elderly. My grandson and his girlfriend worked in our local jail. They were the oldest of my grandchildren and they were all at risk for getting exposed to the dreaded virus. It only gets worse as I continue to feel sorry for myself. My son worked in the legal system, the military, and Law Enforcement.

I found myself crying one day as I thought of how many of my family members were potentially in harm's way. I cried to the Lord one day out of fear and frustration saying, "I raised my kids to be outstanding citizens who have very responsible careers, and this is the thanks I get." I continued with "My kids are out on the front lines where it is dangerous to be. They are needed and considered essential employees. So, because I raised my kids up the right way, they grew up, became educated, and obtained highly responsible careers.

So, I put them on the front lines." Is this the thanks I get Lord?", I asked.

I fumed about this to myself until one day I believed I may have heard from the Lord. He himself was a servant of all mankind. He was perfect in all his ways. He was on the front line for saving all of mankind. Mary did her job raising Jesus and she did a real good job. Now here he was. He was humiliated, cast down and beaten. He was made to carry the full load of mankind all the way to the cross. There he physically suffered at the hands of the cruelest of cruel humankind. The very humankind he was trying to save were killing him. There he gave his life out of duty and out of love. He gave, he died, so you and I may live.

Mother Mary how did you feel? How did you ever manage to get through knowing how much you loved your child, and how much you cared for him and looked after him and got him to adulthood, only to be crucified on the cross of shame? Did you wish you had not have raised him up in the way you did? Did you wish it were anyone's son but yours up there on that cross?

I felt ashamed of myself. I had wished anyone other than my precious children or grandchildren to take care of the sick, needy, injured or elderly. Let someone else's kids do the job I thought. Right? Why can't my kids be the ones sitting at home safe and sound and quarantined from the virus?

Lord, I would ask you please forgive me for my selfishness. My family members took up their cross just as

Jesus took up his. My children chose to serve others as Jesus chose to be a servant to all of mankind. When looking at eternity, they will be awarded gifts for their unselfish service to others. They will be rewarded by another one who gave unselfishly. He was without spot or blemish. He knew no sin. He was love in the flesh as well as God in the flesh. He gave so that we may live. He gave so that we may live to serve others. He gave everything. His name is Jesus. I pray my friend that you would give your heart to Jesus, today, and allow him to direct you in your life journey.

CHAPTER 2

Benefits?

I have known some people still of the working age, to speak fondly of all the benefits they will have when they are old enough to retire. Some work extremely hard for those benefits that are promised to them. Some give up time with family and friends to keep their jobs where they are close to putting in the years required to secure their retirement benefits. Some have worked more than one job, and as much as three jobs, to secure more than one retirement benefit coming in every month once they reach retirement age.

This reminds me of a story Jesus told in the bible found in Luke 12:16-21 where a man had a farm that produced so many good crops, the farmer became rich. It seems like it would have taken a lot of time and effort to make such a great farm. Perhaps he missed time with his family but justified it as we sometimes do today, by putting all his money up for retirement and making his financial future in his old age secure. Matter of fact this farmer that Jesus spoke of, had so much return on his crops, that he had to build a bigger barn to hold it all.

The man was pleased to have enough money stored away for many years to come. He planned on being able to take it easy in his old age. He was looking forward to eating and drinking and being happily satisfied. I do not think there is anything wrong in storing up for our old age, but I am wondering if precious time with family and friends was lost while storing up, or working more than one job, and having even less time in the here and now to enjoy life.

Now enters God in this story of the farmer. God informs the farmer he is to die the very night he hears from God. God asks the farmer who will get all the benefits of his hard work and missed time with friends and family? Is that a question we should be asking of ourselves? God further tells that a person is a fool to store up treasures on Earth and yet not have a relationship with God.

My own personal thought is that I do not think God means you should not plan for your retirement. But maybe we should be careful as to not over work for retirement benefits by giving up a lot of family time or time spent getting to know God. Who knows whether we will live to retirement age? Who knows if all the hard work you are doing for your future will be given to someone else's future?

Shouldn't we be sure we are not working so hard to be all set for the future, that we neglect our time with God, family, or friends in the here and now? What kind of a future do we have without Jesus in it? Are we spending as much time seeking God for ourselves, or teaching our children about God, as we do working for a future we are not guaranteed of here on Earth.

In Matt. 6:33 it tells us to first seek the kingdom of God. Matter of fact the first commandment is to love the Lord your God with all your heart, soul, and mind. Matt. 22:37-40. We are to do everything we do in the name of our Lord, Jesus. We could ask ourselves, are we putting Jesus first while working for our future. Spending time with Jesus is one of the most important things you can do when planning for your future.

CHAPTER 3

Filters

We see pictures of beautiful movie stars, both male and female, who fit the description of beautiful in any dictionary you could ever find. The makeup that is worn hides any imperfection they may have as well as accenting any naturel born beauty they were blessed to be born with. They also add filters on computers and the most unattractive becomes almost beautiful.

When these people have used make up and filters to attract a mate it can be difficult if not sometimes impossible to measure up to the filtered look with the unfiltered. When meeting someone in person who has only seen the filtered you, the person you are meeting may not even recognize you and they may not like seeing the real you. You, in person is not what the pictures promised. In person they get the real you. What you see is what you get, not the filtered or made up you.

Has it ever been like that with you and Jesus? Do you go through the motions of being a person who looks good in church attendance and, helps in church when they need it, yet you have a dirty little secret that you refuse to give up? After all no one is perfect you say. You tell yourself you aren't hurting anyone, and even if you are, they will get over it. Maybe you are too embarrassed to tell anyone, or to get help. Let me tell you something that you may or may not know. Jesus knows all our secrets and imperfections. Those kinds that you cannot filter out or cover up.

Jesus knows our every weakness, our habits good or bad, and yet knowing everything about us, he loves us anyway. He is and always will be willing and able to help you in all your ways. Whether you know it or not, or believe it or not, Jesus is still there for you, and for the whole world.

I have heard of some who would never leave the house without putting make-up on. It was almost as if they did not want anyone to see what they really looked like. Covering up imperfection has been done since the beginning of time. What was the first thing Adam and Eve did when they committed the first sin in the garden of Eden? It was one of the first and biggest cover ups since the beginning of time when they covered up their fleshly nakedness. {Genesis 3:21.} How many times have we tried to cover up something we have done? Have we ever committed a sin while seemingly living the life of a devoted Christian? If so have we tried to cover it up? Trying to cover up the imperfected part of who we really are. The side we battle against. You know, good versus evil. It is a battle that has been going for many years before our time. But can you cover up enough? Can you hide your sins enough? Can you run from Jesus, or hide your sins from him?'

In dealing with crime, we see cover ups all the time. In Politics we often hear of people in positions of power covering up crimes or behavior. Sometimes we find out about the attempted cover-ups, and other times we never completely get the absolute truth of a situation due to the amount of time taken to form an iron clad cover-up. We see in the bible Where David committed adultery and tried to cover up his sin of adultery by committing murder. David's attempt to cover up his act of sin confirmed what he already knew, which is God knows everything and sees everything. There are consequences to sin and to the cover up, as David found out. It is a remarkably interesting story with good morals which can be found in {1 Kings 1 and 2 as well as 2 Samuel 11 and 12.} Those of us who know Jesus, know we cannot hide anything from him. We cannot outrun him and cannot ourselves hide from him. In 1 John 1:9 we read if we confess our sins, he, (Jesus) is faithful and just to forgive us of our sins. He is a forgiving God and abounding in love. (Psalms 86:5)

Once our sins are confessed, and we know he forgives us, we can feel confident that we do not have to concern ourselves about a coverup because our sins have been covered up by the blood of Jesus. (Psalms 32:1) We do not have to feel like we have sinned to much too be forgiven. There is no sin known to man that Jesus will not forgive if we truly repent.

I would love for you to remember today that if we

confess our sins to Jesus, he is faithful and just to forgive us our sins and to cleanse us from all unrighteousness. You can lay down your past right now regardless of how many sins are in it. Jesus loves you unconditionally. Jesus forgives you. Just call out to him. Turn your life over to him and see that the Lord is good.

CHAPTER 4

Prepare and Be Prepared

I was sitting in a doctor's office alone waiting for the doctor to come in. I had left my purse and coat out in the waiting room with my husband since I was just having a quick check up. I was sure I would not be needing my purse or anything in it. While sitting there with nothing to do the Lord was providing not one but two devotionals. But Lord why now? I asked. I'm not prepared to write the words to one devotional let alone two of them. Look Lord, I said respectfully, I have no pen. Both pen and paper are out in the waiting room. The Lord caused me to see that to be ready in season and out of season was not only for preachers and evangelists but for all Christians. Be instant in season and out of season. (2 Timothy 4:2)

I quickly looked around the room and noticed a drawer from which I quickly grabbed a pen. I then looked around the room and found a scrap paper. I feverishly began writing the words that I believed was coming from the Lord. As I wrote I informed the Lord, I will never get it all done before the doctor comes in, but I continued to write. I wrote so fast I could hardly read my own writing.

Several minutes had passed by and my thoughts began

to wonder to the fun filled shopping trip I planned on going to. Then the doctor came in for my checkup. I had not even started my second devotional. I did not know if I could even remember it, but once out of the examination room, I forgot all about my shopping trip. I walked out to the waiting room, grabbed my pen out of my purse, sat down and wrote out the second devotional. The shopping trip would be slightly delayed. Besides, I wanted to put the Lord first above all things. When standing before the Lord to give an account of my life, no friend, no relatives, nor any of my Earthly possessions will be there to help give an account.

What happened that afternoon got me thinking. I wondered how many times we put off things of the Lord. Do we put worldly things before the Lord? Do we spend more time on the internet, playing games, reading social media? How do we spend our time?

There is a story in the bible about putting the Lord first. It is very straight forward about where our loyalties lie. It's found in Matthew 6:33. This verse tells us to seek the kingdom of Heaven first. Matthew 10:38-39 tells us to take up our cross and follow Jesus.

There are more verses that tell us how to live our life for Christ. All it takes is spending some time with Jesus. Spending time in his word. Spending time in prayer. Just putting him first. You will never be sorry, but you will be eternally blessed. While there may be consequences for following Jesus, that is a whole different story for a later time.

CHAPTER 5

Standing Unaware

A young woman struggled with a relationship between herself and her mother. As a child she and her siblings received spankings when it was believed by their parents that someone was breaking house rules. In her own mind she saw her mother as standing by uncaringly as she was spanked by her father. The lady was only a child when she was given spankings with a belt. She and her siblings resented being spanked as children. The past was ruining the future. The young woman a lot of the time, wanted little to do with her mother, and as for her father, their relationship was strained as well. The young woman according to the time frame she was living in now, saw spankings as abuse which was unacceptable, where the time frame the mother lived in saw spankings as the right way to see to it your children grew up to be law abiding citizens.

The young lady was resentful towards her mother, because she saw her mother standing there as she received her spankings while doing nothing to stop them. The young woman saw her mother as neglecting to protect her and her siblings. Over the years this belief built up resentment towards her mother and especially her father who was the one handing out the discipline. Her mother was made aware of how her daughter felt and set out trying to explain to her the difference between today and yesterday in parenting issues. Her mother explained that back in her day when people loved their children, they disciplined them with a belt or paddle. Some parents back in that time period even got switches off the tree and inflicted spankings to the bare legs of their children.

Not till the next generation was it seen as not being the best option for discipline. After all discipline was found in the bible where it says if you spare the rod you do not love your children. (Proverbs 13:24) Simply put, in her mother's day and age it was taught if you love your children you spanked them when they did wrong. You had to tuck away your motherly instinct to protect, and allow the spankings. It was felt by many during that time, if you did not spank your children when they did wrong, you were seen as not really loving them enough.

The young woman just could not understand the real reason her mother was always present for the spankings, and never did anything to stop them. The real reason was that the mother was standing guard over her children. She was there to make sure the spankings handed out by the father did not go too far. She hated having to watch the spankings, but she endured the awful sight to protect them. So, while the child saw her mother as the villain along with her father, the mother was standing guard ready to act as her child's defender should the spankings go too far.

Sometimes people see God as a mean God who stands by and allows unpleasant things to happen to them as a form of punishment. These same people may find themselves asking where God was when the bad thing happened. They may also ask why God did not stop the bad thing from ever happening.

God is always with us regardless of what we may be going through. (Matthew 28:20) God is always there watching over us to ensure whatever is happening does not go too far. (1 Corinthians 10:13) God says there is nothing we cannot handle if we trust in him because he is our strength.

That is exactly what this mother was hoping for as she stood watch over her children. She was believing the discipline would mean that her beloved children would stay clear from a life of crime, drugs, jail, or a long police record. She and generations before her were told, if you love your child, you spank your child when they disobey.

Since that time, we have learned of alternative ways to discipline children. Most of us no longer see spanking as an acceptable form of discipline. We can learn from our mistakes and we can learn from history. We can open our hearts to him and trust him that whatever is happening in our life will be for good in the long run. You can trust in God, the one who sent his son to take the punishment for our sins.

In John 3:16 we read; God loved us so much that he sent his son to bare our sins. "For God so loved the world that he gave his only begotten son, that whosoever believeth in him should not perish, but have everlasting life."

My friend, if you are reading this, and you have not yet asked Jesus into your heart and have not allowed him to guide you through your journey in life, my heart's desire is that you will see the need for that. It will be the biggest, and most important decision you ever make. What you decide, will affect your eternity. An eternity with Jesus is just a prayer away.

CHAPTER 6

Tennants Rights

Ever think of moving? If you are renting your home, ever think of moving and owning your own home instead? I remember moving and I remember it was not fun. Maybe exciting, but moving heavy furniture, and delicate breakables, is not fun.

Once you have found a new home whether it be an apartment or a home, the previous tenant has to move out first before you can even begin to move. Once the previous tenant moves out, the new tenant begins moving in by first cleaning up after the last tenant. You may find some things left behind by the previous tenant that you throw away. You clean up where previous items have been and put your belongings there. You eventually move all your belonging into your new place.

Once all has been completed and your belongings have been moved in, it is now your home. The old tenant has no rights to it any longer. The old tenant gave up any rights to the home the day they moved out. The old tenant does not get to come back to what is your new home.

Like an apartment or home, when you ask Jesus into your heart, it is like moving someone else into a home. That is what happens when you ask Jesus to come into your heart. The devil moves out and the Lord moves in. The important thing to remember is that the devil has moved out. He must move out once you ask Jesus into your heart. Jesus takes over. Jesus cleans things up in your heart. Jesus not only cleans things up but he moves important things into your heart, like a new way of thinking, scriptures to live by and how to love and be a disciple to others.

With you asking Jesus into your heart, the devil moves out and takes with him things such as hatred, hard heartedness, darkness, depression, selfishness, lust, demanding attitude, dishonesty. Jesus gets rid of the way you use to be and gives you a new heart.

Once asking Jesus into your heart Jesus replaces the old former heart with the new, like love, joy, peace, long suffering, patience, forgiveness, integrity, honesty. (Galatians 5:22-26}

Jesus has moved into your heart replacing all the things of the devil. The devil legally has no rights to you anymore. However, the devil being the devil, may change his mind about moving out of your heart and may try to move back in from time to time. He prowls around after moving out, like a lion, seeing if he can still move back or just devour you. (1 Peter 5:8)

Let's say you have moved out of your previous home and into your new home. The previous tenants stop back by about a month later, wanting the home back. You are very content with your new life in your new home. You don't want to move all over again. Of course, your reply to the old tenant would be no way! Hit the road might even be another thing you would reply to the former tenant. As the current tenant, you are perfectly within your rights to refuse entrance to the former tenant. You have the right to ask them to leave, and if they refuse to leave you can then demand it and use legal resources to reinforce your decision. As a new Christian you have the right to refuse to do anything the devil wants you to do. You no longer belong to the devil; you belong to Jesus.

Just as the law would back up your legal rights to remain the current tenants, and refuse the previous tenant's access to your home, the bible backs up your legal right after asking Jesus into your heart, to refuse the devil from returning and trying to persuade you to going back to your old ways. The only way the devil can get you to go back to your previous ways before asking Jesus into your heart is by you giving the devil permission to do so. The devil no longer has a right to you. It is written in the books. Just as we have judges protecting our rights, we have the bible, and Jesus, protecting our rights. In (James 4:7} it clearly says to resist the devil and he will flee from you.

When you ask Jesus into your heart, he moves right in and protects you. Once you have asked Jesus into your heart you have the right as a child of God to live forever in Heaven. Once you have accepted Jesus as your savior, you can live for an eternity in blissfulness with Jesus. The bible, which is the word of God backs you up. Your name is recorded in the lamb's book of life. (Luke 10:17-20} You have all the things you just read in this scripture and so much more.

There is a judge in place and his name is God. He is the judge of all judges. He stands by his written word, and he stands by you 100%. You have the right to say no to anything the devil would offer you. You have the right to resist temptation and the Lord tells you how to resist.

Jesus backs you in every good and perfect thing you do. It's all written out for you in the bible. God who will never let you down. He will always have your best interests at heart, in other words, God has got your back. The devil no longer has any rights to your heart. Your heart belongs to Jesus. Jesus loves you.

When you have questions, you can go to God. You can go to your bible, God's word which guides you in everything you do.

If you have never asked Jesus into your heart, you have a heart full of evil and darkness no matter how good of a person you are perceived to be. You can obtain a clean, perfect heart by asking Jesus into your heart. The second you ask Jesus into your heart Jesus instantly kicks the devil out and makes your heart perfect and new. If you believe in Jesus, you can ask him into your heart right now, right where you are, despite any sin you have committed.

If you already have Jesus in your heart, guard your heart. Keep all filthy things of this current world far away from your heart. You can do that by spending time with Jesus, getting to know him. Jesus, the son of God, was tempted and pursued by the devil. You can run the devil off by using scripture against him. I promise you; you will be happier than you ever thought possible and live better than you ever dreamed of if you ask Jesus into your heart.

CHAPTER 7

Was It Worth It?

I was watching a movie where a young lady in the navy was having an affair with a married man. She was ordered to break it off immediately by one of her superiors. Disregarding orders, she chose to continue the affair. She was eventually caught in the act by the unsuspecting wife. The wife filed charges against the young woman which resulted in the young lady being court martialed and dishonorably discharged. She returned home to her family humiliated and disgraced.

Have you ever done something you knew was wrong from the start? Were there consequences for the wrong you committed? Do you ever wonder if you could go back in time, knowing the outcome of that wrong you committed, would you decide not to commit that particular sin after all?

David in the bible was a man used of God. He overcame many obstacles in his life and became a king. David also committed adultery, and then murder in an indirect way. David also had many concubines or wives, which led to further sin. The result of all those sins committed led to the death of his infant son. (2 Samuel 11-12)

While some people think if you are a Christian,

you never sin, and if you do sin, you are not a very good Christian or you are not a Christian at all. God knows that even if we declare our allegiance to the Lord, that we do still sin. The difference is, we as Christians know we need to repent and try to sin no more. There is an instance in the bible where a woman was caught in the very act of adultery. She was brought to Jesus to be stoned as the law required. Jesus could have condemned her but instead he showed her mercy and forgave her telling her to go and sin no more. It is such a great example of our Lord's mercy. It is found in (John 7:53-8:11) You can have a good relationship with Jesus, and he will never let you down. He is a God of love, peace, and mercy.

CHAPTER 8

Mission Possible

There was a time when I had an especially important recording of a situation where children's welfare was in question. The tape was critical to an upcoming court case. It involved evidence that would prove a parent of wrongdoing against their children. The situation was heading in the direction of the children being in a potentially dangerous environment. The custodial parent was doing their best to protect the children and had hired a well-known attorney who was known for being aggressive with his cases. The tape was a blow-by-blow explanation of just what was going on. I had it recorded on my phone but needed to transfer it over to the computer or some other form so the attorney, and the judge could listen to it.

The parent who was trying to protect the children, along with a close friend tried for a few hours to transfer the tape to an acceptable device but had failed to do so. She was frustrated due to her also trying to get the tape to the right person on the right device. She tried to email a copy of the valuable tape; however, the email was just clocking for what seemed an eternity. She gave up on the email and grew more frustrated. It was an urgent situation due to the safety of the children but also because the parent would be meeting with the attorney, and Judge within the next two days.

The protective parent was disappointed that the evidence could not be used since everything they tried failed to provide a usable version of the recording. She did not want to give up even though the parent thanked her for all she did and suggested they just forget about it. She agreed the parent was right and told them how sorry she was that it did not work out.

That same day that the parent decided to give up getting the tape as evidence, the friend came up with a plan. She did not tell the parent, because she could not give up as they had agreed to do. Her plan was to rush over to a computer company and have them make a copy. She was willing to pay whatever it cost to get a copy of this tape. She was more than ten minutes away from the computer company when she looked at her watch and saw they would be closing in two minutes. She became very frustrated as the tape was needed the next day and by a certain time. Nothing she was trying to do was working. Still, she had the mentality of not giving up, so she made plans to go to the computer company the next day before the protective parent met with the attorney.

Later that evening the friend received a call from the parent thanking her for not giving up because he did receive the email after all with the recording. He was elated and the friend was stunned. When he asked how the friend finally got it to work, she had no answer for him. She had tried to email it but gave up and instead of sending out the email, all her computer would do is clock, so she forgot all about it. It must have eventually worked out without her knowing about it. She was incredibly happy to be of help.

With neither the protective parent nor the friend giving up, everyone involved in protecting the children in question had the evidence they needed to make a very bad wrong, right. In the end it was worth every frustrating minute. They got the prize because they did not give up. The prize being the safety of the children involved.

In Philippians 3:13-14 we are encouraged to press on towards the prize. Whenever there is a difficult situation, you may be facing, press on to reach your goal. Keep your eyes on Jesus and press on. It may not be an easy road, whatever the situation, but don't give up. Move on knowing that your strength comes from the Lord.

CHAPTER 9

A Sponge for Jesus

I was watching a quiz show on television when I heard the definition of a sponge. One of the definitions I found was a person who mooches off other people. I thought about that definition for a short time. I imagined someone as a sponge who always arrives at your house right at dinner time, and after eating their fill, maybe stretches out on your couch for a short nap. They received good food along with the vitamins and minerals their body needed at someone else's expense.

A sponge could also be the person known for borrowing money from people with a kind heart and never paying them back while always promising to. So, we have yet another person who was getting either all or part of or all their financial obligations met at someone else's expense.

Have you ever known someone who was always borrowing things that they never returned or when they did return it, the item was no longer in working condition? Maybe this person had to be contacted over and over regarding returning the borrowed item before bringing the item back. This is another example of someone being able to use someone else's belongings at someone else's expense.

The above-mentioned situations give no thought to how the person they borrowed from worked to earn money to buy the item or items borrowed.

The definition of a sponge is pretty bad. And then I wondered about the positive side of a sponge if there is a positive side and it made me start to think. I wondered if being a sponge could be a good thing if you defined it as being willing to soak up the word of God, and to consume God's word every day. I wondered if reading God's word everyday would cause you to remember it better? If we soaked up the word of God, we could remember it easier, and it would come to mind in the times of trouble. We could receive vital bits of unlimited knowledge, helping us to know how to be strong and maintain a healthy physical and spiritual lifestyle.

Each of us owe a debt that we cannot not repay. God sent Jesus his only begotten son to completely pay that debt on the cross and we benefit greatly from his sacrifice for our sin debt. Our sins have been forgiven and we have been set free. Celebrate eternal life with Jesus because of what he did.

Sometimes it is good to be a sponge if you are soaking up the word of God. God's word has the answer for every situation you will ever find yourself in.

CHAPTER 10

Modern Day Jesus

My chemotherapy treatment was scheduled on a Tuesday in January. We were playing games the Monday night before, just myself, Fred, and April our daughter. While playing games, my daughter April had a seizure. Fred my husband began praying for her immediately and together we pleaded the blood of Jesus over her. Together we gently lowered her to the floor. She had had a grand maul seizure. Once getting her to the floor we began looking for her medication when she had a second grand maul seizure which was way worse than the first one. April began to turn purple, and I began to consider starting C.P.R. when suddenly, she gasped for air and started to breath once again. We cradled our precious daughter for a few short moments and together we were able to get her into the car, and to the local hospital emergency room.

Once arriving at the hospital April had yet a third seizure. Hospital personnel took over for us giving her oxygen, and immediate medication. She had a very high heart rate. This concerned the doctor and he decided to keep her in the hospital for a few days until she could be stabilized.

I cried a lot during the next few days that she lay in the

hospital. "Where are you God?" I cried out in despair. I had so many questions for God and not all of them were very nice. I asked God again and again, over, and over where he was when we were crying out to him for help and why did April have to keep having seizures.

Thankfully after a few days our daughter was released from the hospital and recovered from the seizures she had gone through. The Lord did indeed keep her safe and she got to come back home to us.

It was a few days later when I sat down to watch one of my favorite old shows, The Rifle Man. It was an episode I had already watched several times, but I decided to watch it again even though I already knew how it ended.

As I watched the scene coming up it involved a young man getting slightly injured. I was right there watching what I had already seen before. I knew the young man was going to be okay, so I was not upset at all. I was calm because I knew he would be okay. I did turn my head though while the injury was taking place, but I was still there. I knew what that young kid was going through was necessary for his becoming a much better person because of it. Growth often involves pain. God knows this and is willing to stand beside us through physical and mental pain knowing we will be the better for having gone through it at the end. The all-important factor here is, he knows we will be okay. He knows we will end up better for having gone through it and the most important factor of all is that God is always with us. Through the fire God remains.

Instantly what came to mind was, when I asked before, where were you God the night we called out for you. When Fred rebuked the devil and while I pleaded the blood of Jesus over April, April continued to have seizures one right after the other. Then it came to me, Just as I was there, Jesus was there. Just as I knew the boy on television would be okay, Jesus knew April would be okay. Jesus knows the ending to each one of our stories. Just as I knew it would be okay for that young man in the end, Jesus knows it will be okay in the end for April, and for anyone of us who have put our trust in the Lord. He is there with us during the hard times. He does not leave us and does not forsake us. Jesus knows our ending. He knows we will be okay in the end.

This made me feel better, Knowing God is always with me, through all things. (Joshua 1:9 and Isaiah 12:2)

Is there something you are going through right now? Is it a situation where you cry out to God for his presence and help? Are you wondering where God is in all that you are going through? Are you asking yourself if God is watching you while you suffer through this situation? Perhaps you are questioning why God is not helping you out more.

After reading the story I just wrote about, is it possible for you to see that perhaps the Lord is allowing you to go through the situation, knowing full well you will be okay, and not just okay, but even stronger. It reminds me of having to go through some type of surgery to correct a physical problem. No one really wants to go through all that comes with the surgery itself, but once coming through the surgery, the healing begins, and you feel so much better when the healing is complete.

The bible tells us we will have trials in this life, but Jesus will always be with us. He loves us enough to want us to be stronger than we ever thought possible. With God all things are possible. Can you trust God to walk with you, to guide and direct your paths making you stronger through Christ Jesus?

CHAPTER 11

Good Turned Bad
Turned Good

By choice I was a stay-at-home mom. I loved my children and feared them going out into the world and trying to be good Christians without making every attempt possible to equip them with everything they needed to remain strong in Christ. I wanted to make sure I had done everything I could to help them make it to heaven. I was so thankful to Jesus for all he had done for us on Calvary, and I wanted to give all I could to make sure my precious children knew of Jesus inside and out.

My husband worked full time. I worked at home doing the cooking and cleaning. We were by no means rich, but I made every attempt to take care of their most important needs. I felt that having Jesus all over in their lives was the most important thing I could do. I also wanted to shield them from the wrongs of the world for as long as I could. This thinking is what led me to the thought of enrolling all five of my children in a Christian school. I did not know how we would afford it, but we would just have to make it work somehow.

I pooled what money we had to pay the Christian school

first. Only after paying the monthly fee for the Christian school did we then pay the house payment, utilities, groceries, and our everyday family needs. We did not have it easy, but both their father and I felt the sacrifices were necessary and worth the benefits of our most precious children attending a Christian school. We felt we were in step with what the Lord wanted for each one of our children.

For years our children grew in the Lord while attending the Christian school. Every sacrifice we made was more than worth it to keep them protected from the world and filled with the word of God and how to apply it in their lives. Our children were involved in playing basketball, both boys and girls. They played volleyball, as well. Between our four daughters and one son, we were kept very busy attending almost all their games, and of course the victory dinners afterwards. We supported our children one hundred percent.

Our first three daughters graduated from that Christian school. We looked forward to our other children doing the same. It was right around that time that we began to hear of things we did not like. Once they graduated from that Christian school, our daughters then explained to us, that our one and only son was being beat up almost every day by some older bullies. They did not feel they could say much to us while attending the school because the parents of the bullies worked at the school. One of my daughters did break up the bullying when she observed it going on, but it continued to happen whether she saw it or not. We were also informed our children were viewed as being poor and were made fun of because they did not think my children's clothes were as good as the ones the bullies were wearing.

I questioned my son as to the truth of the situation and he hesitantly confirmed the beating up and bullying was true. I immediately transferred my son and remaining daughter to a different school. I had asked God the why's of the situation. I told God I thought I was doing the utmost best for my children. I told God I had felt my children were safe from bullying since the children at the Christian school were mostly all Christians. Having them in a Christian school did not keep them away from meeting bad people and being treated badly.

I never thought about how Jesus had said we as his children were not part of the world, but just visitors passing through. (1 Chronicles 29:15) His home was in Heaven and so is ours. People hated Jesus because he told them where he came from. Jesus lived an upright life and never sinned and even had sinners as his friends. Jesus showed only love and mercy and grace and yet they tried his whole life to find fault with him. It did not matter what they tried to find; they never found any fault within him. The bible also says, if they hated Jesus who never, ever, did anything wrong, why would they not hate us as Christ followers. (John 15:18-25)

I am confident that even though my children had their struggles with ill-behaved children in that Christian school, they still were taught the word of God. Not only did we go to church on Sundays to hear the word of God, but they also got it almost every day in school. We also as a family had devotions and praise and worship almost every evening. God's word did not fall wasted to the ground. The bible says that God works out everything for the good of all those who love him, and he did no less than that in our case.

After the bullies had grown and were out on their own, I heard they had become somewhat involved with drugs, and the physical abuse they handed out as children, continued into their adult years when one of them were arrested for physical abuse of their spouse. While my children may not be 100% perfect, they have all grown to be responsible adults, with especially important jobs, and to this day remain faithful to the Lord. The most important thing I have ever wanted for my children, was that they know the Lord, love the Lord, and serve the Lord, and ending up with Jesus in Heaven.

I hope somehow this devotional book helps to show you what kind of a Godly life you can lead. God is so good, and he loved the world so much, that he gave his only son whom he loved, to become a sacrifice on the cross for us. If you were to give your heart to the Lord Jesus Christ, you would never want to live another day without him.

CHAPTER 12

Who Me?

I am no more important than the next person. I have my ups and downs and sometimes I don't act like a child of God should act. Even while being a Christian husband and Christian wife, my husband and I sometimes get upset with each other and have our short-lived spats. I remember once in our marriage my husband and I had been arguing off and on for a few days. Those few days of disagreeing with my husband left me feeling sad and weepy on the inside while I was trying to act normal on the outside. I did not feel like being normal when all I wanted to do was to go hide somewhere until it all blew over. To make matters worse it was cold, dreary, and raining outside. Then without even expecting it, right in the middle of my gloominess I received two devotions from the Lord. I was surprised when I got the one devotion because although I had gone to church that day, and had been praying, I still felt saddened. But after I received the first one, and was done writing down notes for the first devotional, a second devotional came. I was pleasantly surprised that the Lord was using me despite the way I was feeling.

God used people in the bible even when they were

showing defects in the way they were thinking or acting. God used broken and flawed people. We are never to broken for God to use for his purpose. God used a King who committed adultery, and murder, a Hebrew with a speech defect, he used a prostitute, a tax collector, and many more imperfect people.

After I was done writing the two devotionals the Lord gave me, I was getting ready to join my family in some fun activities when the Lord supplied me with a third devotional. After the third devotion I was like, Okay Lord go right ahead and give me as many devotionals as you please. I am your servant, and I am your worthy servant because you have made me worthy.

I believe Lord wanted to show me something and I would like to share it with you. You see I think sometimes we think we're not worthy, or we think we just don't know how to help people. I would like for you to see that the Lord can still use us no matter what situation we are in. We may make mistakes, but God can still use us. God tells us to share the Gospel of Jesus Christ. Mark 16:15.

2 Timothy 2:24-26; Acts 10:42; Matthew 28:19-20 are just a few verses telling us to share the gospel.

Jesus is not just my Savior; he is my friend. Because he loves me, I love him and want to share the good news. My wish is that through my devotionals I could help even just one or a million people to know my Jesus and for them to walk in the light and love of Jesus.

CHAPTER 13

Holy Interruptions

We were driving down the road on a beautiful sunshiny day. We were meeting our family for one of my precious grandchild's birthdays. It was an outside facility filled with fun things to do as you build wonderfully beautiful memories. Just as we were getting close to the facility, we had previously been warned about not being late due to regulations of the facility so we planned on getting there early. Not far away from the facility a beautiful white dog and Brown dog walked in front of us on a busy highway. They narrowly missed getting hit by more than one car. I gasped for air and my heart sunk as I pulled over to see if I could get them. I was on a mission to remove them from harm's way.

My husband was focused on getting to the facility so we would not be late, while I was focused on getting the dogs and saving their lives. I went against what my husband wanted to do. He wanted to keep going but I could not do it. I could not keep going. My heart broke for those poor helpless dogs whose lives were in danger. I began to cry as I turned to my husband and said, "We have to save their lives." I pulled into someone's driveway but could not catch either one of the dogs. They were scared and they were hungry, but fear overtook them, and they ran away from us. I backed out of the driveway into the busy highway once again, but I was looking and searching for those dogs to make sure they didn't get close to the road again. My husband informed me of how I should put getting to the party on time instead of rescuing some stray dogs. I wondered if maybe I was acting childish, so I told myself oh well, at least I tried. It was just as I was giving up the search when out of corner of my eye, I saw movement far away. It was the two dogs. They were in a field across the road again and they were headed back to the highway.I pulled into a different driveway and this time my husband was very upset with me and I busted out crying. I couldn't keep how I was feeling inside anymore. I said to my husband, "But I have the chance to save a life, and I'm going to do it."

As the dogs approached the car, the white dog came up to me, but the brown dog crossed the busy highway again narrowly missing getting hit. I found a tag on the dog. The dog was very thirsty, weak, and tired. I did not know how long he had been on the run.

I could not catch the other dog, so I said a word of prayer for its safety and headed to the party with the dog we found, sitting on my husband's lap. Once we arrived at the party, we got the dog some water, and we read the tags on his collar. We called the owners telling them we had one of their dogs, and where we were. They told us that their dogs had gotten out of the fence and ran away. They were so happy we found at least one of their dogs.

It only took a few minutes for them to get to us. After expressing gratitude once more, they took the dog loaded him up in their car and headed for home.

Later, after the party, my husband called the people once again to see how the dog that we found was doing, and to see what happened to the other dog. The owners informed my husband that the other dog had found its way home safe and sound. We were awfully glad to hear that the dogs were back home safe and sound. All the trouble I went through to save those dogs proved more than worth it.

Once we returned home, I thought about all we had been through earlier that day. It reminded me of how Jesus pursues us When we are lost. Is my heart the same as the heart of Jesus? He not only pursues us, but he also died on the cross for our sins. There is no greater sacrifice. Since he did that, we can be an example of Christ's love to others and direct them to the Lord Jesus. We could ask ourselves; "Do we go out of our way to win people to Jesus?" I hope when I get to heaven there will be people there because I took the time to show them Jesus.

CHAPTER 14

Holidays

It was one week before we got together as a family. I started getting ready way before Thanksgiving because I knew time would go by fast and Christmas would be here before knew it. I had jewelry boxes, pillows, hats, and blankets to make, along with putting down a new floor in our dining room. All of this on top of everyday cleaning and laundry that screamed to be done every single day.

I love having everyone here at Christmas time and I needed to have everything done as close to perfection as I could get it. After all, new boyfriends, and new girlfriends of my grandchildren were going to be there for the first time.

Part of our Christmas gathering would be a white elephant gift exchange for all the adults, and a Christmas program put on by several of my grandchildren. They would sing, read scripture, play games and this year we would have my grandson playing his tuba.

There would be tons of deserts and snacks to nibble on all afternoon. There would be about 24 loved ones here opening approximately 75 gifts or more.

Before any gift opening, the traditional reading from the bible, the story of the birth of Jesus which was read by my husband just as he had done when our children were young. We made sure our family knew that Jesus was the reason for the season and not just Santa. I am not a Santa hater. I would like to have him pay for all the gifts and wrap them and keep track of who has what under the tree.

During one of my busy times, I was looking at all I had to do and wanted to do, yet I was not getting anything done fast enough or good enough. I was also losing some of the things I bought and needed. I was upset with myself to the point of tears being shed out of pure frustration.

I told my husband I needed to pray as I shut the bedroom door behind me. I fell on the bed crying and praying. I told the Lord, I loved him and could not do this without him and pleaded for his guidance and help.

During this prayer I saw an image of a dog going in circles chasing its tail. He was going amazingly fast yet going nowhere and getting nothing done. That was me alright.

So many times, as Christians we have to go here or go there, do this do that and before we know it days have gone by and we had no time left to read our bibles or even pray.

Taking time to pray and ask for my Saviors help gave me time to calm down.

I started weeding out my must do list and I was calmer about the whole situation.

I thank Jesus for being the go-to man for help in everything we do.

Please make time for Jesus. You will be better off

spending time with him. The Holidays will pass just like everything else on Earth. Some of the gifts will be forgotten over time, along with other holiday celebrations. One thing that will not be forgotten is the time you spend with Jesus, or the day you ask Jesus into your heart. I have heard many a pastor say that when you ask Jesus into your heart, there is a new name written down in glory, and that name is yours. Revelation 3:5, Revelation 21:27, and Luke 10:20 are just a few scriptures that mention your name being written in the book of life.

May God bless you and keep you in all your ways.

CHAPTER 15

My Tribute to Jodi Koeppel

There is a nurse in blue. In a split second before I can remember, I look to see if it is my Jodi working this night. Quickly I remember with sadness, Jodi is not with us anymore. When I go to the hospital, when I go to the doctor's office, or sometimes at the grocery store getting groceries, I see nurses in blue. Every time I see one of these nurses, I quickly think of Jodi.

Jodi Koeppel was a true angel who came to Earth for a short time. Too short a time for those who knew her, and for those of us who came to love her. She was a beautiful brunette with angelic blue eyes. When she smiled, her face lit up as well as the whole room she was standing in. She worked full time in the local emergency room where she experienced the good with the bad of caring for others.

Jodi always tried to see the good in people, but sometimes being nice was a bit difficult, when it came to people who hurt little children. She loved little children. She loved her two girls and when she married her husband, she loved his two daughters as her own. She was the kind of mother who would read the bible to her youngest daughter when she was afraid. She cared unselfishly for her teenage daughter who was born with a lifelong illness. She drove many miles to a specialty hospital to make sure her daughter got the best of care, without missing any time from work or time with the family. She grew protective of her four daughters if she thought someone may not treating them fairly. She cared deeply for people in pain and would put her own feelings and well-being aside to care for others. She worked for our hometown hospital, a world renown football team, and had just started to work for the county jail. Despite all the work she did to help support the family of six, she never missed a beat when it came time to taking care of her husband or their children. I had never seen her husband's eyes light up like they did when he was with her. The love they shared was truly a God given love. Not only did her husband love her deeply, but her children did as well. It was because of her loving and giving heart that she took time to read the bible to them when they were afraid of thunderstorms. That is just one of the many, many examples of the Christian character, that Jodi possessed.

Then one day out of the blue Jodi was gone. Taken from her devoted husband and family, she worked tirelessly up to two days before she passed from here to Heaven. No one not even herself realized how sick she was when she checked into the hospital one afternoon after passing out. But just the same, she left, quickly and without warning. But she did not leave without leaving memories. She left even more than that. She left behind examples of how to live a life serving others, so much so she became a very important part of our lives. It makes me wonder, when it comes to Jesus, and my relationship with him, what kind of impression will I leave behind when I leave here to go to Heaven.

By giving our hearts and lives to Jesus, he has made a way for us to spend an eternity with him in a most unimaginable heavenly home. In that place with Jesus, we can be with our family forever. I look forward to seeing Jodi again and to never having to say goodbye. She was an angel while she was here on Earth, but she is truly an angel in Heaven.

One important thing Jodi taught me was that I should make time to visit my loved ones. Spending quality time with my loved ones may hopefully leave good memories with them. I do not think we should take for granted our loved ones since none of us are guaranteed tomorrow. Enjoy being with your loved ones. I think we should be sure and not allow hurt feelings, or angry feeling to keep us a part. Be willing to forgive quickly and exchange words of kindness. Sharing love and hugs may be a much better way of leaving the gathering of our family or friends.

I remember my last time being with my Jodi. I was visiting her in the hospital and getting to tell her I loved her. As I was leaving her that day, I leaned over and gave her a hug. I then took her hand as I said a prayer for her. I am so glad our last time together was of such a loving and caring time together.

I love you Jodi and I always will.

We should all work for the good of others, while loving the Lord, Jesus Christ. Would you read Philippians 2:3, 1 John 4:21, and 1 John 4:11, and allow the Lord to lead you into action.

CHAPTER 16

Our Own Way

I was shopping at our local secondhand store, and I found a lot of stuff to buy, even though I had only intended to window shop. It was taking me a long time to shop since I was finding a lot of stuff and I needed to compare prices, colors, sizes, and weigh the benefits of getting it and not getting it. This shopping trip had taken me over an hour of walking from one side of the store to another, and up one isle then down another. Once I had something picked out, I had to decide whether I really needed it or not. I had to decide whether I was being frivolous or not with my intended selection.

When I was finally done shopping, I was on my way up to check-out and along the way I had found even more items of interest. Almost the whole time I was shopping there was this little boy who looked to be around two years of age, who was with his grandmother. This toddler was continuing to scream out so loud, that it echoed around the entire store. All the while he was screaming, he was pointing towards the toy section and grunting very loudly in between screams. In addition, between the screaming and grunting I heard his grandmother say to him that she was not going to buy him a toy if he did not stop acting out and screaming. I must have heard her say this to the boy in between his screaming and grunting, at least twenty times.

I found myself wanting to walk over to them both and politely explain to her that I was an old lady from old school and what that child needed was not a toy but a gentle and loving swat on his fanny. I knew the grandmother was not serious about her threat, and I knew in the end that the little boy would get the toy he wanted from his grandma whether he behaved himself or not. I sort of figured he knew that as well. The screaming and grunting were driving me to near craziness, so I decided to call it a day from shopping and headed for the check out.

It ended up that both the grandma and the child checked out at the same time as I did only at a different cash register. In the grandmother's cart was indeed the toy for the screaming boy. I was so proud of myself for predicting how this whole situation would end up. However, when the two walked out of the store, there was no toy going with them. I wondered where the toy went but figured it was all for the best. I still heard the screaming and while he was catching his breath, I heard the grandmother tell him she just did not have enough money. I found myself thinking he did not need the toy anyway the way he was acting.

I carried my many bags out to the car and began loading them up. It was then the grandmother and the boy walked towards me. The grandmother then began explaining how badly the boy wanted a toy and she was one dollar short, and did I have a dollar to spare so she could go back into the store and buy the toy. I explained to her after apologizing, that I did not ever carry cash and that I only had my banking card with me. As the woman was walking back into the store, I was thinking but wait a minute, I have change I could spare. I would not mind giving the lady the change, but I thought wait a minute, if I give her the change I would be contributing to the delinquency of a toddler. So, I did not say anything as she disappeared into the store.

As I was driving away, I saw the same lady and child leaving the store once again with the child holding the toy. I wondered how they managed to get the dollar needed for the toy, but I was not curious enough to ask. I started to wonder if I should feel bad for being stingy, but it was too late because we were driving away from the store.

As I was leaving the parking lot, I was provided a very good question from the Lord. Could that spoiled child be acting the same way I sometimes act when requesting something from the Lord, whether it be a beautiful house, boat, car, or important career. How many of us, including me get upset with God when something does not go the way we want it to. Do we get angry with God and just not speak to him for a while? Do we say things to God or about God out of anger or frustration? Are we behaving this way in hopes of getting what we want from God? Do we think we deserve to have what we ask for since God is in control and we are his children? If things do not go our way, do we blame God and whine and complain? Are we hoping to change God's mind ending up with what we wanted to begin with?

If God was to give me everything, I asked for no matter what I did or said, I would truly be a spoiled kingdom kid. Would God withhold good things from me just to teach me a lesson or to guide me in the right direction?

If we think about it, God may withhold things from us because it is not appropriate, or it is not the right time. We may not always get what we ask for, and if we don't do we throw our own kind of fits? God's ways are not always our ways, but God knows what is best for us. In Jeremiah 29:11 "For I know the plans I have for you declares the Lord, plans to prosper you, and not to harm you, plans to give you hope and a future."

We can trust God to know what is best for us. God sent his son to die on the cross for our sins, because he loves us and because he was doing what is best for us. God will always be there with us and will defend us and never leave us. My heart's desire is for everyone reading this devotional to be trusting in the Lord and having the Lord live in their hearts.

CHAPTER 17

The Watcher

There was a wonderful young lady who was a very dear person. She loved making people happy and loved making sure her family and her extended family were well taken care of. She even made sure her ex-husband was given gifts on his birthday and special holidays. She had a heart of compassion for everyone. She was loved by everyone.

This dear precious young lady had flashbacks of her childhood which were scarring her from deep within. She remembered getting spankings from her adoptive father. They were violent spankings according to her memories. One of the things that made her almost bitter towards her mother was the picture she had of her mother just standing by watching her husband hand out spankings. She did nothing but watch. While the child getting a spanking was crying, and trying to endure the harsh spanking, the mother stood by silently.

Over the years resentment built up towards her father but especially towards her mother. I mean after all wasn't a mother supposed to protect her children from spankings such as this. Her mother always told her and her siblings that she loved them, but if this was love, then she would rather not have it. She chose to not be close to her mother. She saw love a different way. She did not want to be the kind of parent her parents were. She wanted to demonstrate love for her children in a different way.

Her mother tried to explain to her that back in the days where she herself was being raised spankings were the way you showed you loved your children. You loved your children enough to spank them to keep them from living a life of sin. In other words, if you did not spank your children when they disobeyed it was your fault if they grew up to be hoodlums. After all her mother herself had received many a spanking back in her childhood days.

After this child reached adulthood, along with her siblings, it was then that the day of spanking for the act of disobedience became the thing not to do. Doctors were writing about new ways to discipline without using spankings. Spankings were found to be some form of abuse if injury resulted from the spankings. It was then taught it was best not to use the spanking method at all.

In speaking with this woman's mother, the pain of the possibility that she was seen as abusing her children that she loved so deeply, caused her to wonder if she knew what love was at all. After spending much time reliving the situation it became clear to her that she was standing guard so to speak. She stood nearby observing the spankings with her heart near breaking. None the less whenever she was home, she stood by every spanking session watching, and watching.

She told her husband when enough was enough if she felt he may go too far. Her heart may be breaking but she remained at the scene. She was there to make sure the spankings never ended up with injuries. She would allow spankings because she loved her children and wanted them all to respect rules, and laws, and to abide by them all. Regardless of how the spankings broke her heart, she stood her ground and watched over her children. At that era of time, spanking your child was not viewed as abuse, but as needed discipline.

In life today some people see God as a big mean God because he seemingly lets things happen to them and they ask why. Sometimes they wonder what God was doing while something was happening to them. God is always there with us even when we go through the bad stuff, but God is standing over us making sure it does not go further than what we are able to bear. In Nehemiah 8:10, it tells us the Lord is our strength. In Isaiah 41:10, it also tells us to not fear because God is with us, and God will strengthen us and help us. He is always with us. He will hold us with his right hand. In Psalms 121:5-8, We are told that the Lord watches over us, and he will watch over our life, and that he will also watch over our coming and going.

God's ways are higher than our ways. But both cared for the ones they were watching over. Both were watching to be sure no more was given than could be endured. God makes a way for us to endure. He knows of our opportunity to grow from our experiences and to help others endure life's difficult moments. That is like what this young mother was hoping for. Hoping that if she allowed the spankings to take place, which were inwardly breaking her heart, the children she loved would grow up to be law abiding citizens and responsible adults.

These parents did in time raise their children to be all they had hoped for them to be, and then some. Yet it was not without a high cost. The cost of losing the love and respect of one or two of their most precious children seemed a high price to pay for doing what was supposed to be the right thing to do.

Would this child ever know how hard it was for her mother to stand watch over her children? Would this child ever understand the heartache the mother felt having to watch the spankings their children endured along with her children's tears and moans and groans? She allowed it out of love for children. She endured it out of love. Would she ever know beyond a shadow of a doubt, that it was supposed to have been the right thing to do?

We can learn from our mistakes, and we can learn from history. We can learn straight from Jesus himself, if we but open our hearts to him, and trust him through whatever is happening in our life. There will never be any disappointment in God, who sent his son Jesus to die on the cross for your sins. In John 3:16 we are told God sent his son to die on the cross for sins. Jesus willingly died for us, and he did so out of love.

What can we do for others to show them the love of God?

CHAPTER 18

Turn on the GPS

My husband and I were traveling in a city we were not familiar with. We had been in an accident through no fault of our own. The insurance company provided us a rental and it was time to take the car back. I was sure I knew how to get to the desired location. My husband was following behind me in his car since we both had to end up at the same destination. Between using the GPS on my phone and having my husband following me, I felt confident in finding the desired location. Between traffic lights and lunch time traffic, my husband and I got separated. I became very frustrated when we ended up going in different directions. I began to feel lost when I could no longer follow the GPS due to traffic flow and lane changes. To make matters worse my husband was gone somewhere, but where?

The feeling of being lost was bad enough as I was in heavy traffic which did not leave much time to look for streets, or businesses. I felt lost and alone. The feeling of being lost, alone, and not knowing for certain what street to turn on was almost too much to bear. I was beginning to feel very anxious while trying to remain calm. It was a terrible feeling. I hate being lost anywhere.

I imagine that could be similar to someone being lost spiritually, in that they do not Jesus. Imagine living in this world where good looks and finely tuned body shapes are regarded as one of the important things to have in life. A life where people are often judged by outward appearances. Being lost with trying to obtain things that are forever out of your reach. Being lost yet trying to find the right lifetime partner, in hopes that together you may come to some direction for your lives. Finding the right lifetime partner may lead you in the direction of having a family. Perhaps your children can achieve in life what you have not been able to. Perhaps your children can provide you with a lifetime of love and affection. Who knows what direction having children may lead you in. But you do not know for sure where they may lead you, depending on whether they grow up being a good kid or a kid who consistently makes bad choices. You may not even feel like going in that direction.

Some people know not what direction to go. They go to alcohol to get away. They go to drugs to feel better about themselves and anything else they feel lost over. Some people seeking directions for their life attempt to find it by several different personal relationships, even after they are married.

There are many different ways lost people use in hopes of finding their way in this world. Even if they feel they have arrived at their desired location, that feeling may not last long if something else in their life does not lead them to feeling fulfilled. Lost people are seeking for directions. Directions for their life and even directions for life after life.

The bible talks about lost people. In Matthew 6:25-26 we are encouraged to not be so concerned over clothing, food, or drink. Isaiah 41:10 tells us to not fear or be dismayed, for God will give us strength and will help us. We have the Lord with us, and he will never leave us. We will not be lost or without direction for our life if we invite Jesus in our heart to travel with us through life. If we follow in the direction, he leads us we will be satisfied with whatever we have.

The only lasting direction we need is to follow Jesus, because one place he leads us is beside still waters Psalms 23. If we follow Jesus, he will show us great and mighty things. Isaiah 30:21. Jesus will direct or lead us into all truth, and this truth will set you free. John 16:13.

CHAPTER 19

Shadows

We rescued this adorable looking black chihuahua. Her name is Molly Jo. She was in a very loving home where she would never want for the rest of her life. All her needs were not only met, but she was pampered and spoiled like an only child.

Molly loved going outside to play. This was great because her beloved owner loved being outside as well. There was a garden with a beautiful pond filled with all kinds of water life. There were chickens and there were ducks. Her owner was all about celebrating life. Anything's life whether it be insect or animal she loved and respected life even in something other than human life. This was bliss in its finest order for animals of any kind.

How quickly things can change. After coming home one day from a day of shopping, Molly and the other dog was let outside while groceries were put away. Tired and looking forward to resting, once everything had been put away, the dogs were called back into the house. Something caught the eye of the owner and she walked outside to a horror scene. Some of her pet chickens had been mauled and killed. One chicken especially caused much distress because it was not just another chicken, but a beloved family pet. The only evidence the owner had was that Molly was the only one with blood on her mouth and chin. Her owner could not believe it. Not Molly. Molly had never shown any sign of being aggressive. The owner just would not believe it. Some other animal had to have jumped the fence and committed the terrible crime. Still the owner decided to watch Molly from now on when she went outside even though the whole yard was fenced in. Things were quiet at the house once again and things went back to normal.

Normal that is until one day her owner came home to find once of their favorite kittens dead. This time there was no doubt who committed this crime. It was Molly. There was blood all over the house and on little black Molly. Words cannot describe the pain and suffering that came with having to clean the house of the mess all the while knowing she could never let this happen again. Now that she knew it was Molly, without a doubt, something had to be done.

It was decided that Molly could never be trusted with animals smaller than her again. Molly was surrendered to us since we had dogs and most of them bigger than Molly. Would she ever live that name down? She still exhibited the tendency to dominate and attack other dogs. She just could not hurt them, and she backed down. She was never given the chance to hurt the vulnerable dogs.

Molly eventually earned the love of her new family.

However, we could never let our guard down with her. A few years had gone since the killings, yet Molly could not live down her past. She was still referred to by some as "Chicken Killer", and some still did not like her because of her past.

Her previous owner missed Molly and visited Molly showing her much love and affection. Molly was used to her new family, but always enjoyed the visits. Molly had settled down as she aged a couple of years. Still, her past followed her. Molly had not killed since she moved into her new home. She was still an overly aggressive dog as she still attempted to intimidate the other dogs in the home. Through all this she was still loved by her previous owner as well as her new owners.

Molly has a hard time leaving her past in the past. It reminds me of people in the bible who did things in their past and once making changes to their life, still had trouble leaving whatever deeds they committed behind them.

Moses who was used by God, had a past of killing of an Egyptian who was caught beating a Hebrew. Moses even ran away to avoid punishment for the act. Exodus 2:11-15.

A great man of God was David. He too had a past he would rather not be remembered by. He saw a beautiful woman taking a bath. He had her husband who was serving as a soldier killed by proxy. He then married the woman and he already had at least seven other wives making this woman his eighth wife. Murder and greed were his deed.

Yet he was used of God after leaving all that in his past. 2 Samuel 11-12.

There is a story of a harlot who had things in her past while living as a harlot that she would rather everyone forget. However, she was also used of God in a big way. You can read about it in Joshua 2:9-13.

I too have a past I would rather forget. I have in my past, committed deeds that I knew were wrong, while claiming Jesus as my Lord and Savior. I gave into temptations of the flesh. I repented from those sins. While Jesus has forgiven me, and forgotten the deeds, people have not. I am relieved that Jesus forgave me and scattered those sins as far as the East is from the West. Psalms 103:12

I pray anyone reading this would take time to examine their lives. I pray if you have not yet received Jesus as your precious Lord and Savior, that you would take the time to invite him into your heart. I pray you allow him to scatter your sins as far as the East is from the West, so they no longer exist as part of your new life. You can start over. Jesus gives a new start every morning. Regardless of the acts of sins you have previously committed, they do not have to be a part of your past, present, or future. Jesus is quieting knocking on your heart's door. Will you open your heart to Jesus?

CHAPTER 20

※

Treasures

The house of an elderly woman and everything in it would be left to her children and grandchildren when she passed from this life to eternity. What would they find when it was time to sort all the treasures she had saved? She had a reason for keeping everything, and everything was special to her because of the memories they held.

First there was the collection of her favorite movie, The Wizard of Oz. Some of the collection was bought for her by family members that were near and dear to her. The figurines, books, pictures, and records each held special memories of happy times.

In the collection were many large stuffed animals, and some of them were incredibly soft, which comforted her as she held them. To the elderly woman her stuffed animals created an atmosphere of love and acceptance. Holding one or more of the stuffed animals represented hugs and warm thoughts.

There were books on several bookshelves. There were so many books on the bookshelves, that at first glance, it looked like a small personal library. Having all the books provided a wealth of knowledge there at her fingertips whenever she chose to read them.

Another part of the house looked like a well-stocked country store. Gift wrap was found piled nearly reaching to the ceiling. Food of all kinds were found in the cabinets and there was enough to feed a small family for a month. This gave her the security she needed to feel confident, she would never have to go without again like she did when she was a young mother.

Can the things of this world really bring you peace? Can hugging a stuffed animal bring you peace? If so, how long will that peace last? The collections of different objects seem to comfort her. How long will that comfort last? While I do not think there is anything wrong with collecting objects and them having a special place in your heart, one may find out those moments of peace, or happiness they bring may not last for very long.

Do we as mere human beings seek peace? A peace that becomes a part of you. What about comfort? Is there ever a time when you needed to be comforted? Where do we run for peace or comfort?

I know of a for sure place that you can find peace and comfort. It is in the arms of Jesus, or in the Bible which is him speaking to us. I feel so good when I am in need of being comforted and I pick up the Bible and read, "For he himself is our peace, and the peace of God, which surpasses all understanding, will guard your hearts and your minds in Christ Jesus." Philippians 4:7

Jesus gives us a kind of peace that we can only get from him. Jesus tells us "Peace I leave with you; my peace I give to you. Not as the world gives do I give to you. Let not your heart be troubled, neither let them be afraid." John 14:27

If we search the word of God, we will find true peace. "And let the peace of Christ rule in your hearts, to which indeed you were called in one body." Colossians 3:15

When we find ourselves in a situation that we need to be comforted we can find comfort in the words of Jesus as well. "The Lord is close to the broken hearted." Psalm 34:18 "He heals the broken hearted and binds up their wounds." Psalm 147:3

There are so many more verses that bring peace and comfort. Matter of fact everything we are going through can be helped by reading God's word. I pray you would be comforted in every situation you may find yourself in, and that you will find everlasting peace in all you do.

My friend, Jesus IS the answer.

CHAPTER 21

Love Abounding

One Sunday our pastor was praying the opening prayer when he mentioned how God does not see us, his child, or as an insecure person. He went on to say God sees us as his child. He loves us no matter what.

As a parent you love your children because they are your child. You may have a child who is top of their class, and you are so happy over all their accomplishments. You are happy for them, and you see nothing but a bright future for them filled with countless opportunities.

Then you may have a child who struggles with everything that comes his way, and on a daily bases. Accomplishments come hard for this child even though they try their very hardest.

You also have a child who does not seem to care if they achieve in life. You find yourself having to constantly find ways to motivate them in everything they set their mind to do. You do your best to motivate them only to find out that all you have done to encourage this child seemed to have been a waste of your time.

It is easy to love the child who is successful at anything that comes his way. You love your children regardless of any wins or loses in their life. Your love is not a teeter totter, loving them when they are successful and not loving them when they fail. No, you love them no matter what they do or don't do.

As for the child who continues to struggle in many different areas. You choose to love them through the ups and downs. You love them through their failures and successes. You are there for them when maybe no one else is. The love of a parent knows no bounds. Most humans have an extraordinarily strong bond with their children.

I know of a stronger bond than that of any human bond. We have a Heavenly Father who loves us because we are his child. His love is not because of anything we have done. Matter of fact we do not deserve his love, nor is there anything we can do ourselves to earn his love. God just loves us, and he loves us the way we are. God has loved us since the beginning of time. He loved us enough to send his son Jesus to die on the cross for our sins. He loves us enough to make a way for us to live with him forever in Heaven. You can call God, the highest power of the whole the universe, since the beginning of time, Father. (John 3:16) Just as Jesus is God's child, if we accept Jesus as our Savior, we too can become a child of God. Jesus will forgive you of any sin you have ever committed if you confess them and ask forgiveness. There is no sin he will not forgive if you ask for forgiveness. Once you are willing to ask for forgiveness of your sin, and ask Jesus into your heart, you can confess Jesus as your Lord and Savior. Having Jesus as your Lord and Savior affords you many things. First, it gives you love that knows no bounds, along with Peace and joy and everlasting life with him in blissful happiness.

I hope to see you there in Heaven one day, and when we meet, you can tell me what you thought of my book. Until then, won't you ask Jesus into your heart my friend? You will not be sorry. He is waiting for you. He loves you with an everlasting love.

CHAPTER 22

Cell Phone Madness

I have several family members who are rarely seen without their cell phone. I have seen some of them on their cell phone up until the second they leave for destination. Once arriving at their destination, they pull out their cell phone once again. I have even seen people in church using their cell phones.

I am sure you have heard of people using their cell phones while driving and due to their lack of concentration towards their driving end up causing an accident. Sometimes they injure themselves and at other times they are responsible for injuring others. It could even be more tragic resulting g in loss of a life.

I heard someone say once "I don't know what I'd ever do without my cell phone!" I've heard another unbelievable comment such as, "I'd feel stark naked without my cell phone." Even I feel safer with my cell phone while out in public. Sometimes I ask myself what did we ever do before cell phones?

After observing the great use of cell phones made me wonder What it would be like if we used every waking moment reading our bibles instead of searching the internet.

How much better would we be at getting along with others. How would it be if when we got to someone's house, we whipped out our bible and read it instead of the cell phone.

How about when we want to do something to avoid boredom, we opened our bibles and read it instead of scrolling on our phone, or playing games on our phone.

It appears that the cell phone has taken over our lives. We turn to them for wisdom, knowledge, directions in traveling and more. If we turned to God and read his word asking him for wisdom, and knowledge, you can be sure you would receive it.

If we did not want to get bored so we pulled out a bible and read it, we could benefit much more. If the whole world spent as much time reading their bible as they spend on their phone this would be a very different. We would know God so much better. We would be Heavenly minded.

Dear Lord, help us to be closer to you in every way. Help us to remember to spend more time with you than any Earthly thing. It is you that redeems us. It is you that died for our sins that we may live eternally with you. Thank you, Lord, for your great love and eternal love towards us. In Jesus name Amen.

CHAPTER 23

Comfort

I was lying in bed surrounded by all my beloved fur babies laying very close to me. I was taking my medication before getting up to face the day with all of its many different challenges.

It was so comfortable and cozy in my nice warm bed with all my fur babies cuddling me. Not all of them are cuddly though. I noticed at the foot of my bed one of my smaller fur babies was up scratching at the blankets on the bed trying to get them made into a comfy little spot on the bed.

After watching her for a few minutes, I found myself wondering why she was not lying next to me in her usual spot. I looked around and saw that my bag of medication was laying in the spot where she usually lays so I moved it. As she continued to dig and tug at the blankets, I patted the bed where her special spot on the bed was. She looked up at me as I called her name. Hopping and jumping over her siblings, blankets, and stuffed animal she came to rest at my side as she laid down next to me.

She quietly got comfortable and taking a deep sigh, laid her head down to rest. Within only one minute or maybe two minutes she was fast asleep. I wondered if we as humans were like that. Trying to find comfort outside of and away from the ultimate comforter. How often are we found trying to comfort ourselves with the things of this world instead of running to the ultimate comforter. How many times do we seek comfort from a bottle of alcohol, cigarettes, or drugs? These have the potential for causing us harm and possibly death.

God is calling us daily to come to him through his word and by praying, so we may be comforted. We need to try and leave behind the things of the Earth that we think brings us comfort and run to Jesus. Let the words Jesus speaks to us comfort us above anything else we may or may not have.

2 Corinthians 1:3 Says, "Praise be to the God and Father of our Lord Jesus Christ, the Father of compassion." It speaks of God as a God of comfort and that he comforts us in our trouble. It goes on to say that he comforts us and wants us to comfort others when we see them in distress.

Romans 8:37-38 tells us we are more than conquerors if we trust in God. God is able to delivers us and comfort us in all things. We only need to trust him.

I like the verse found in John 16:33 that assures us we can have peace in this world. God is always with us and encourages us to not be discouraged because he will strengthen us and help us.

There are so many more verses in the bible to encourage us and give us directions for living a life with Jesus at our side. With Jesus at our side giving us strength and encouragement and peace, what have we to fear? Not that it is always easy, but God's word remains true. We do have the God of comfort by our side daily and he is there for us. We just need to trust him and call out to him. He will be there for you.

CHAPTER 24

Having It Out with the One You Love

Fred and I were having it out one day. His jeep wasn't running right for one thing. There was more than one thing wrong with it and each thing would be very expensive to fix. To add to all of those expenses there were the everyday and every month expenses. To top everything off he accidently permanently ruined his phone which meant having to replace it which was not in our budget. During all of this I was feeling overwhelmed with trying to manage all our financial burdens.

Being so on edge made me less willing to talk things over. My husband had different ideas than I on how to work out all our financial issues. We each thought we were right, and the other was wrong. We each felt it had to be done our way. There was no room for discussion since we both thought we were right. Neither one of us would listen to the other.

So, after a rather loud voicing of our opinions, our determination to fix our situation our own way, we in anger departed ways to do our own separate household chores. As I got my chores done, I was still angry about what had happened earlier, and I did not feel like saying I was sorry and make up with my husband.

Later that evening as I was finishing up on my end of chores, I began to feel sad and just generally out of sorts. My husband called from work to thank me for the new phone I had bought him earlier that day and we both apologized for our childish behavior. The apology did not take away my sadness.

I sought out my scripture key for bible verses that would be like medicine to my spirit and soul. I read 1 John 4:4; Psalm 55:22; Isaiah 59:1; and Psalms 103:3. It came to me as I was reading how much I loved all of my children. Each one was different from the other, yet I loved them all the same. It began to dawn on me how God must feel when his children like Fred and I have such heated disagreements. He loves us all just the same. His heart must be saddened to see two of his beloved family members attacking each other with such unkind words.

Knowing how sad he must be to see his beloved children arguing, I also began thinking of how happy he must be when two of his children who were once quarreling, have decided to ask forgiveness for their arguing and are now getting along once again.

I wonder if we should remember when you are at odds with a loved one, it is not just you who is sad about it. I think it is a good feeling to remember that when we have put aside our differences with that loved one, there is someone else who is happy. It is our Lord and Savior Jesus Christ.

Printed in the United States
by Baker & Taylor Publisher Services